Daily Jewels:

Aligning Your Crown as a Daughter of the King.

Ashley Shepherd

DEDICATION

This book is dedicated to all of the sweet daughters of the King in our Beautifully Designed community. It has been the biggest blessing to come alongside you in your walk with Jesus Christ. I pray that you wake up every morning with purpose as you straighten up your crown. Always remember how loved you are by the ONE who beautifully designed you.

ACKNOWLEDGMENTS

Thank you to my amazing husband, Ryan, and my champion boys, Wilson and Levi. You always encourage me to live my dreams and remind me how strong I am because of Jesus. I love living out our Kingdom purpose in the beautiful Smoky Mountains together.

Daily Jewels:

Aligning your crown as a daughter of the King.

Have you ever looked in the mirror and said, "Who am I, and what is my purpose?" As women we have many roles and responsibilities and it's easy to forget who we really are. Sometimes, our identity can get wrapped up in our performance at work, how well our children behave, or how many likes we get on social media. When we put our identity in these things, we will always walk away defeated and feeling not enough. In the Fall of 2017, I wrote a book on identity, if you haven't read it, check it out at www.beautifullydesigned.com/book. It will take you on a journey of replacing negative labels with God's Truth and will help you go deeper in God's Word.

Whatever season of life you are in, I can guarantee you have a to do list and are facing some sort of giant. If you are not waking up and looking in the mirror and saying, "I am amazing and was created for greatness," then I want you to dive into these daily jewels with an open heart because your Heavenly Father wants to remind you that you were created for a specific purpose.

In the Bible, God has many names; Judge, King, Light, Redeemer, Shepherd, the I Am, and so many more. My favorite name He holds is FATHER! There is so much safety and security in knowing we have a Heavenly Father that not only created us perfectly, but also sent His son, Jesus, to die on the cross for us. Then, He raised His son from the dead to give us life. If you believe that Jesus is alive and in your heart, then you never have to wonder WHO(SE) you are. If this is the first time you have heard about Jesus or have questions please visit...

www.beautifullydesigned.com/meetjesus.

The cross changes everything, now we don't have to put our identity in being the best mom, the perfect co-worker, or grandmother of the year. Those are just roles God blessed us with. He renamed us on the cross, HIS DAUGHTER.

In today's society we have immediate access to so many other voices and opinions, so it's easy to forget our Heavenly Father's voice. Over the next 30 days, I pray that you start to hear His voice because He is calling His daughters to rise above the noise and start living the life He beautifully designed for you. The first thing I want you to do is straighten up your crown; some of you have totally forgotten you have one on. Each day you will be picking up another "jewel" to add to your crown so you can grow brave as you face the day. Join me on a treasure hunt to discover the extraordinary jewels that are hidden in the ordinary places. You are royalty, beloved, and a daughter to the King of Kings, the Savior of the world.

Because you are a (daughter), God sent the Spirit of his Son into your heart, the Spirit who calls out "Abba, Father." So, you are no longer a slave, but a (daughter), God has made you an heir. -Galatians 4:6-7 (emphasis added)

CONTENTS

Day 1: Brave Enough

Brave: ready to face and endure danger or pain; showing courage.

Have you ever been in a situation where you have to choose whether or not to be brave? Maybe it's a job offer, new relationship, growing your family, or maybe it's just facing a conflict in your life. Every week I usually face a situation where I have to choose bravery over fear. Honestly, there are weeks I get exhausted trying to muster up the energy and right attitude to choose bravery. Sometimes it's just being brave enough to not flip out when my boys jump on their dirt bikes or ride the zip line their daddy built. Then there are other days I am dealing with a difficult personality and I have to be brave enough to keep my mouth shut. As women, we juggle a million things daily, and the thought of being brave for it all can be overwhelming. What are you facing right now that requires you to be brave? Are you ready to endure it showing courage?

My boys love the Narnia movies, so we watch them over and over. The other day there was a line in the movie that jumped out at me. Lucy is around 8 years old and she just learned that she has to face a battle. She is asked if she is brave enough to face an enemy being a female. Lucy lets him know quickly that she thinks that she can be brave enough. Those two words "brave enough" made my heart leap. I immediately felt the Lord whisper "stop trying to be brave for everything." I woke up the next morning with a little less weight on my shoulders because I didn't feel like I needed the courage and strength for everything. I just had to be "brave enough" for what was next. I grabbed my Bible and not my phone because I knew that without Jesus' words and truth in my heart I couldn't face the day.

The source of our bravery and energy to be courageous can only come from the One who created us so perfectly. God knows our gifts, flaws, and imperfections and He wants to fill our hearts up and give us His strength to endure the danger and pain with courage. Rise up beloved daughter of the King, you are BRAVE because of your Heavenly Father. Let's talk to Him.

Daily Prayer:

Heavenly Daddy,

Help me face this day with YOUR bravery and strength. As I face all of my conversations, decisions, and situations, whisper words to my heart. I only have courage because I know that You created me for great things. If I have to endure any pain or danger today, allow the Holy Spirit to take over and help me rise up to face it with courage and love. Thank You for giving me the strength I need in every situation. I put my trust in You, Jesus! In Jesus' name.

Love,

Your Daughter

Daily Jewels:

"Be strong and courageous, and do the work. Do not be afraid or discouraged, for the LORD God, my God is with you. He will not fail you or forsake you until all the work for the service of the temple of the LORD is finished." 1 Chronicles 28:20

"Finally, be strong in the Lord and in his mighty power." Ephesians 6:10

"Be strong and let your heart take courage, all you who hope in the LORD." Psalm 31:24

Daily Reflections:

_____

_____

_____

_____

_____

_____

_____

_____

Don't forget your crown today!

Day 2: Guiltless Nap

Rest: cease work or movement in order to relax, refresh oneself, or recover strength.

Are you the type of person that loves planners? I am not good at making lists but I love buying pretty planners. In our culture it's the norm to have every second filled in our planners. There have been mornings I dreaded the day because I knew there wasn't much time to breathe. I have the habit of feeling useless if I am not productive. When I do have a few minutes, I find myself "scrolling" on social media. A few weeks ago I found myself feeling anxious and overwhelmed, so I called one of my mentors and she asked me if I had "rested" recently. I was silent, because I knew in my heart the answer was no.

I have seen a common thread with women who stay busy; the second they aren't, they feel guilty. Why is that? Why do we feel the need to have a full calendar that leaves zero time for us to be renewed and refreshed? This very morning, I woke up at 10:30 am, and my immediate thought was "wow I am lazy." But if I reflected back to the last 2 weeks I went NON STOP. Why do we think we must justify the need for our rest? Society makes us feel "lazy" if we take time for ourselves. So many of us will choose to listen to those voices and run ourselves ragged because we don't want to seem unproductive.

Your day or week may be making you feel anxious, so I want to encourage you to stop and open your Bible. I believe in the midst of our chaos we need more than just sleep, we need God's supernatural rest. My friend and founder of Her Voice Movement, Jenny Donnelly, released a video series on REST. She has encouraged me and thousands of other women to

R-Release E-Every S-Single T-Thing to the ONE who created it all. I want to encourage you to make time for your Heavenly Father so that He can help rest your soul and keep you focused on the things that matter. I truly believe if we leave space in our day to rest, we would find the time to release every single thing to Him; therefore gaining His Peace in the midst of our to do list. Let's start today by talking to our Heavenly Father.

Daily Prayer:

Heavenly Daddy,

Help me take a time audit of my day today. Reveal to me the times I need to stop what I am doing and focus on what YOU are doing. Help me find those moments of "rest" where I can release every single thing to You. I know You can refresh my heart and mind to tackle anything. Remind me today and every day that I can REST in YOU, my Daddy, the King of Kings. My "to do list" will not overwhelm my become list; help me to become the daughter of the King you beautifully designed. In Jesus' name.

Love,

Your daughter

Daily Jewels:

"Come to me, all you who are weary and burdened, and I will give you rest. Take my yoke upon you and learn from me, for I am gentle and humble in heart, and you will find rest for your souls." Mathew 11:28-29

"Do not be anxious about anything, but in every situation, by prayer and petition, with thanksgiving, present your requests to God. And the peace of God, which transcends all understanding, will guard your hearts and your minds in Christ Jesus." Philippians 4:6-7

*If you want to dive deeper into being "Still" and finding "rest," you can go to www.hervoicemovement.com and click the Still tab. The study and video series will walk you through an amazing journey of resting in God.

Daily Reflections:

_____

_____

_____

_____

_____

Don't forget your crown today!

Day 3: Stop Screaming at Me

Loud: producing or capable of producing much noise; easily audible.

Do you remember back in the day when your TV would mess up and it made a horrible loud noise with white snow all over your screen? Maybe I am showing my age, but every time this happened I would run to the TV to turn it off because it was so loud and obnoxious! Sometimes I think many of us are walking around with white noise in our head, while we strive to be everything to everyone.

Maybe you are in college hearing and seeing what others are doing and you shift your priorities to look like theirs. You could be in your mid-thirties, like me, raising kids and looking around at how all the other moms are making it look so easy. Maybe you are retired and the noise you were used to is gone. Every season has a new noise, so I want you to reflect on the day ahead. What noises are coming? Is it opinions of co-workers, baby coos, phones ringing, children playing, or keys on the keyboard? Right now I am listening to our loud dryer dry the clothes for the 5th time because I hate actually folding them. The dryer has one purpose- to dry my clothes. And as you face the day, guess what, you have one purpose. It's easy to complicate what that could be because we all have responsibilities we "think" are our purpose.

Try this exercise. Set an alarm on your phone for 6 minutes. Close your eyes and try to clear your mind. Just sit in the quiet. (I will wait here).

I hope you participated in this exercise because I just showed you what your purpose was, to stop. Your Heavenly Father wants to whisper His still small voice to your heart.

He wants to show you things. He wants to direct your steps, and we have to learn to drown out the white noises of life. If you have never heard His voice, I want to ask you a simple question: Have you made time and cleared your mind and heart long enough to hear? Start there, and if you want to learn more, I encourage you to order Priscilla Shirer's book "Discerning the Voice of God." This book changed my life.

Growing up, my daddy would call my name and "how" he said it would help me determine if I was in trouble or if he just needed something. I saw my daddy everyday so I could recognize his voice out of 100 other men without actually seeing him. Your Heavenly Father is waiting on you to eliminate what is drowning Him out, so He can become louder. Let's begin our day with prayer and remind our hearts that our purpose is to grow our relationship with our Heavenly Father. The rest will fall into place according to His will.

Daily Prayer:

Heavenly Daddy,

I am about to face the day with many noises, so my prayer is that You help me learn to be quiet. There are so many things screaming at me, and it can feel overwhelming. Help me discern what is white noise and what is YOU speaking to me. I know my purpose is draw close to You and You will fill in all of the details. Help me to trust you MORE! In Jesus' name.

Love,

Your daughter

Daily Jewels:

"For you are my rock and my fortress; For Your name's sake you will lead me and guide me." Psalm 31:33

"Make me walk in the path of your commandments, for I delight in it." Psalm 119:35

"Teach me to do your will, for you are my God; Let Your good Spirit lead me on level ground." Psalm 143:10

Daily Reflections:

_____

_____

_____

_____

_____

_____

_____

_____

_____

Don't forget your crown today!

Day 4: Love Me, Love Me Not

Like: having the same characteristics or qualities as; similar to.

I love people! I truly do! My husband says when I see someone I know, I "force hug" them. He reminds me all the time that not everyone likes to hug. Well, that is just crazy to me. That gentle reminder came in handy when I recently found out that one of my "friends" didn't like me. What? I will never forget the first time I walked in the room and she ignored me like the plague. I had no clue why, so I spent two days wondering what in the world I had done or said. The thoughts consumed me and made me feel anxious.

I believe every woman, regardless of her age, has experienced something similar. I picked up the phone and called one of my prayer mentors. This was the beginning of growing in a deeper relationship with Jesus Christ. As much as I love "hugging," I also love "fixing." I wanted to pick up the phone to "defend" myself and figure it out because the thought of someone not liking me hurt my heart. My mentor shifted the conversation from "her" to why the feeling of rejection consumed "me."

Have you ever felt rejection or been in awkward social situations where you don't know how people feel about you? I began a journey of realizing that I put all of my safety and security in other people. She directed me to Psalm 139 "Search MY heart O God........." The reality is, I never gave God a chance to search my heart because I was trying to figure the other person's. I was so consumed with where their heart posture was, I was ignoring mine. When I prayed I realized that what people think about me is their opinion, as long as I am being obedient to the Lord then that should be my only concern. God is my defender, but in the past I never gave Him a chance to defend. I want to encourage you to open up the book of Psalms and read it aloud. You will start to see that you can have the discipline of silence because God is fighting for you.

As you start this day, I want you to ask God to "search your heart." Rejection hurts but it does not define you, your Heavenly Father does.

Daily Prayer:

Heavenly Daddy,

I pray that as I go throughout the day You remind me of how much You love me. There are people out there who love me as well as people who don't. Help me focus on the ones who love and support me, the ones You have put in my life to encourage and draw me close to You. Help me find my value in our relationship only. You are the only One who will never leave nor forsake me. In Jesus' name.

Love,

Your daughter

Daily Jewels:

"Keep your life free from love of money, and be content with what you have, for he has said, "I will never leave you nor forsake you." Hebrews 13:5

"but God shows his love for us in that while we were still sinners, Christ died for us." Romans 5:8

"For am I now seeking the approval of man, or of God? Or am I trying to please man? If I were still trying to please man, I would not be a servant of Christ." Galatians 1:10

Daily Reflections:

_____

_____

_____

_____

_____

_____

_____

Don't forget your crown today!

Day 5: Dress Rehearsal

Dress Rehearsal: the final rehearsal of a live show, in which everything is done, as it would be in a real performance.

I grew up loving theater. I performed all the way through college. I loved taking a character and becoming it for a short time. But what I loved most was "dress rehearsal," because that was what made me confident for opening night. We would be able to work out the kinks and practice until we got it. There are many days where I wish we had a dress rehearsal in life. We would be able to "practice" at a job before we decided if we liked it. Maybe we could even hang out with someone with no emotions before we called them "friend," that way nobody ever got hurt. Wouldn't it be awesome to have a glimpse of what is coming next in your life so you could perfect it when it came to real life?

I have struggled with insecurity for years, mostly because I don't like the unknown. In my late 20's as I was raising my young boys and I remember journaling and asking God to "give me a sign." I had no idea where He wanted to me serve, work, or who to grow a relationship with. I was barely surviving the laundry, and I didn't know my next step. I was in a "waiting room," but the Lord quickly revealed to me that it was a "preparation room." The reality is this life is NOT a dress rehearsal. I have spent different seasons struggling, and even depressed, because I wasn't confident in what was coming next. I truly believe I have missed some God moments because of my attitude and insecurity. God was there the whole time, wanting to show me the way.

Have you ever felt this way? Have you ever felt insecure of the unknown? Waiting doesn't mean you are inactive, it means you are developing. The power of God is in the process, and sometimes the preparation room is the only place where we can train our minds, hearts, and souls. Your purpose in life is not to find the "next" thing to pursue or how to gain more followers. Your purpose actually has nothing to do with you and everything to do with how God can use the gifts He has given you. The waiting room is for training, so grab some snacks and Bible and get ready to learn how to use everything God intimately woven inside you when you were in your mother's womb.

If you focus on God and patiently prepare, the next door will open and you will be ready for whatever it has for you. Ladies, sometimes we need to focus on the people sitting with us in the waiting instead of what we are missing. The small conversations, quick smiles at the grocery store, encouraging texts can be the exact purpose God has for you today. Look up, prepare, and be ready to be developed into everything God has for you.

We don't get to practice or perfect something before we try it. This is where we have to choose to trust God. If He showed you what the next week looked like, you wouldn't talk to Him or trust Him because you would already "know." Let's ask the Lord what we need to learn and grow through during this season to help us to the next one.

Daily Prayer:

Heavenly daddy,

I pray You can help shift my mindset when I am in a season of "waiting." Help me focus on developing into the woman You called me to be instead of the "next door" that could open. You are the door and I pray I walk right inside of Your arms through Your Word and prayer. My purpose is You,

Jesus. I pray I can encourage someone that is in the waiting and remind him or her God is preparing them for great things. Thank You Jesus for every season and for being in the process, I trust that You are doing a good work in me. In Jesus' name.

Love,

Your daughter

Daily Jewels:

"Why, you do not even know what will happen tomorrow. What is your life? You are a mist that appears for a little while and then vanishes." James 4:14

"And I am sure of this, that he who began a good work in you will bring it to completion at the day of Jesus Christ." Philippians 1:6

"Wait for the Lord; be strong, and let your heart take courage; wait for the Lord!" Psalm 27:14

Daily Reflections:

_____

_____

_____

_____

_____

_____

_____

_____

_____

_____

_____

_____

_____

Don't forget your crown today!

Day 6: The Dreaded Mirror

Mirror: a reflective surface, now typically of glass coated with a metal amalgam that reflects a clear image.

I have a confession to make: at night when I have to change clothes and take my make up off, I will only turn my closet light on so I can barely see myself. The dents in my legs, wrinkles under my eyes, and stretch marks on my belly make me want to throw up. I have made a habit of using the words "fat, ugly, plain, old, and gross" when I see what is reflected back and there are just some nights I don't want to face it. You can basically say, "I beat myself up."

Typing this brings tears to my eyes, because it truly matters what we believe about ourselves. Today's culture puts so much pressure on women to not just carry and have children, but that they have to look like super models doing it. Society has made it the norm to Botox, fill, and change to hide our imperfections. I spent years wearing a sweater in 90-degree weather because I felt uncomfortable and just wanted to hide.

The feeling of wanting to be invisible consumed me, until God showed me in Genesis that "We were created in His image." I read that scripture one day and the Lord gently said, "Stop bashing me." I knew I needed to change the way I saw myself but I didn't know how. God began to reveal different stories in the Bible to me. My favorite one is about the woman who bled. She had to hide because the people thought they would contract her disease. The doctors couldn't heal her, so she went to find Jesus. She could only get close enough to touch the end of his garment. And the second she did, she was healed. God called her out, and after she told everyone of her healing (how brave of her), He renamed her. God said, "DAUGHTER, your faith has made you well." This is the only time Jesus uses the word Daughter in the Bible. (You can read more of the story in Luke 8).

We have to seek Jesus, ladies, just like the woman who bled did and allow Him to heal us from the inside out. We have created habits in our lives that bash what God created so perfectly. We have to stop worrying about our imperfections and start thanking him that each wrinkle represents wisdom, and each stretch mark represents life. Get around people who encourage and love you, because it matters who you surround yourself with. Ask yourself if you would be ok if your children said those things about themselves in the mirror? Let's model to our children, nieces/nephews, or grandchildren what it looks like to be confident even in our imperfections, because we are ROYALTY!

Daily Prayer:

Heavenly Daddy,

I pray in Jesus name that every time I look in the mirror I see myself through Your eyes. Help me Lord not to believe the lies I whisper to myself, and help me re define beautiful by focusing on Your image. Help me make a habit of seeing my crown over my imperfections. You make me whole and perfect Jesus. Help me be a confident role model to the children and people I influence. In Jesus' name.

Love,

Your daughter

Daily Jewels:

"So God created mankind in his own image, in the image of God he created them; male and female he created them." Genesis 1:27

"For you created my inmost being; you knit me together in my mother's womb. I praise you because I am fearfully and wonderfully made; your works are wonderful, I know that full well." Psalm 139:13-14

"For the Lord will be your confidence and will keep your foot from being caught." Proverbs 3:26

Daily Reflections:

_____

_____

_____

_____

_____

_____

_____

_____

Don't forget your crown today!

Day 7: Don't Grow Weary

Weariness: extreme tiredness; fatigue: reluctance to see or experience any more of something:

Have you ever woken up and immediately counted down the hours until bedtime again? Nope, just me? Well, let me explain myself. I may physically feel tired but the right word is "weary," which means EXTREME fatigue, which causes reluctance. The need to do "all the things" as women, oh and you have to look good doing it, oh wait, and don't forget to sign up to volunteer for EVERYTHING. Please make sure to work out and eat a salad, and one last thing, please make sure your kids have groceries and clean underwear EVERYDAY! Even typing that exhausted me!!

When there is so much going on, it's easy to grow weary. Usually when my weariness settles, my heart unsettles and I don't feel good enough for anyone. I also need some counseling on how to say "no," because I am the queen of "squeezing" everything in even when I am going crazy. I also love to "start" MANY things but never actually finish anything. Can you relate?

In 2017 I was going through a season where I felt weary about everything, even the parts of my life that were blessed. The laundry even overwhelmed me. I had a conference to attend and I almost backed out last minute because it was just another "thing." As I prayed, I felt the Lord nudge me to go. When I walked in, they had us put away our phones, grab a yoga mat, our Bibles, and journal. The worship was amazing, but the best part of this whole conference was the opportunity to experience Jesus. It was just Jesus, me, and incredible men and women of God filling my cup. I was on my knees praying and asking God to help me not feel so weary and worn out, and I heard these 2 words: "Stop striving." It was plain as day! The definition of striving is, "make great efforts to achieve or obtain something." My heart started beating fast because in that moment I realized I was striving over everything (my job, my marriage, my ministry, my parenting). I was striving so hard for everything to succeed and to be perfect that I strived myself right into weariness.

I let go that day. I opened up my arms and gave everything to my Heavenly Father. It was never supposed to be mine to carry. I had the weight of perfection, keeping up with social media, and the need to succeed pressing down on my heart. I crumbled into the arms of Jesus, and my life has never been the same since. Do you feel weary today? He has a purpose, and that purpose was never meant to be perfection wrapped up in a pretty bow. He is with you, with His arms wide open, ready to take the burdens and weight that was never meant for you. You are so loved!

Daily Prayer:

Heavenly Daddy,

I feel weary and I need You today! I need You to help me stop striving and just start looking to YOU! I know that with You, You love me in spite of me, and You are there waiting to carry the weight that was never meant for me. I can truly be me with You, Father God. Please renew my mind and give me strength to face my day. Help me be still in Your presence and experience all of the LOVE and GRACE You have for me. I am imperfect and beautiful in your eyes! In Jesus' name.

Love,
Your daughter

Daily Jewels:

"So let us come boldly to the throne of our gracious God. There we will receive his mercy, and we will find grace to help us when we need it most." Hebrews 4:16

"Cast all your anxiety on Him because he cares for you." 1 Peter 5:7

"Look to the Lord and his strength; seek his face always." Psalm 105:4

"But he said to me, 'My grace is sufficient for you, for my power is made perfect in weakness.' Therefore I will boast all the more gladly of my weaknesses, so that the power of Christ may rest on me." 2 Corinthians 12:9

Daily Reflections:

_____

_____

_____

_____

_____

_____

_____

_____

_____

_____

_____

_____

_____

_____

_____

Don't forget your crown today!

Day 8: Help My Unbelief

Belief: an acceptance that a statement is true or that something exists.

The other night we took the boys to the baseball fields. It was cloudy but we thought we had time to hit some balls. Well, we were wrong. It started raining buckets, so we had to run to our car and rush home. The storm started raging with lightning and thunder. When we got home, our little dog was curled up by the door looking scared. As we walked in the house I felt the Lord say, "I knew this was coming, even if you didn't." It doesn't matter what season of life that you are in, there are always storms. It could be sickness, depression, exhaustion, big decisions, and even tragedies. Every season has some kind of storm, but that day God did something in my heart that helped my unbelief.

Have you read the story of unbelief in the Bible? Check out Mark 9 about a man's son with an unclean spirit inside of him and how he desperately wanted a miracle. The disciples tried to cast it out but it didn't work. When Jesus came to the scene, everything changed. He is the HOPE of the world. The father wanted his son healed so he told Jesus, "But if you can do anything, have compassion on us and help us. And Jesus said to him, 'if you can!' All things are possible for one who believes." Immediately the father of the child cried out and said, "**I believe; help my unbelief!**"

This story gives me so much hope! There are so many times in my life when I trust the Lord in a storm, but I have a sense of unbelief through my "worry and anxiety" over it. Take a deep breath sweet daughter, because it's ok to have unbelief.

It truly shows the neediness you have for your Savior. Jesus shows us in this miracle that through our belief in HIM anything is possible. Are you expectant that the Lord can work a miracle in the midst of your storm or are your eyes fixed on the raging waves? Turn your eyes away from the situation and fix them on your Savior.

Remember God has already gone before you and He is not surprised about anything. He is the one that flung the universe into existence. Grab your Bible then read about His miracles, and let the Hope rise up in your heart that He is doing a miracle in your life, because you are HIS daughter! Let's pray to get this day started.

Daily Prayer:

Heavenly Daddy,

I believe in you, Jesus, but please help my unbelief. Close those holes in my mind and heart that allows doubt, worry, and anxiety to creep in. Lord, help me be expectant and for my eyes to be open to see the miracles You are showing me in my life. Thank you for already going before me, and for Your provision in the midst of my storm. Help me trust in Your plan for my life, and help me to stop taking control. I pray I can see You over the storm. I love you, Jesus, thank You for always being there and never changing. In Jesus' name.

Love,

Your Daughter

Daily Jewels:

"If you can! All things are possible for one who believes." Immediately the father of the child cried out and said, "I believe; help my unbelief!" Mark 9:23-25

"And he said to them, "Why are you afraid, O you of little faith?" Then he rose and rebuked the winds and the sea, and there was a great calm." Matthew 8:26

He said to them, "Because of your little faith. For truly, I say to you, if you have faith like a grain of mustard seed, you will say to this mountain, 'Move from here to there,' and it will move, and nothing will be impossible for you." Matthew 17:20

Daily Reflections:

_____

_____

_____

_____

_____

_____

_____

Don't forget your crown today!

Day 9: Pruning

Pruning: to cut off or cut back parts of for better shape or more fruitful growth.

I love a new year, it's always an opportunity to set new goals and begin new in so many areas of life. I used to set myself up for failure by having too many goals in the busy seasons of my life. I remember one year feeling like the biggest failure because I didn't stay committed to a particular workout schedule that honestly Richard Simmons probably couldn't keep up with it (if you aren't sure who he is Google him, you will thank me later). As I was praying about my goals in January 2018 I heard God whisper, "this is the year to slow down to speed up." I got excited because, remember, I like to rest (read the devotion on the Guiltless Nap). But by month 2, I realized I was headed into a pruning season that would force me to wake up one day where everything looked unfamiliar.

I don't know if you have ever experienced a pruning, but it's just like when you take scissors, walk up to a plant, and cut off the things that aren't bearing fruit. It's painful, and God slowly revealed to me that He wasn't just pruning the things in my life not bearing fruit (selfishness and pride as an example). He was also going to prune good things out of my life. In John chapter 15 verse 2, Jesus explains to His disciples that,

"Every branch that does not bear fruit, he takes away, and every branch that does bear fruit he prunes, that it may bear much fruit."

I will be honest, in the midst of God removing people from my life, face to face with conflict, and having to take a stand for WHO I am, I felt WEARY. I wondered if I would ever see the "fruit" Jesus talked about in John 15. I remember crying out to God one night begging Him to just give me a taste of the fruit. I don't even need a whole banana, just let me have a bite. I was tired of trying to prove myself or the future God had planned for me. Then one night, I heard HIS voice; the still small one that gives you chills through your whole body. He said, "I AM THE FRUIT."

My heart shifted, my mind stopped wondering and I made a decision that day to stop focusing on what God was pruning out of my life. I started feeding what was ALIVE, and that was Jesus Christ. I knew I was in the valley ALONE, but I was gaining all of the nutrients, love, and encouragement from my Heavenly Father. So I dug my heels in the dirt, I began to pray, dive into God's Word, and eat the fruit He so richly gave through His Word.

I began climbing out of the valley seeing that the purpose of it all was to give me time to slow down so that I can know my Heavenly Father in a more intimate way. And one thing I have learned is that HE is my defender. He is my strength and the lifter of my head.

I want you to open your Bibles and read John 15. Ask the Holy Spirit to speak to you through His Word. We are either in a pruning season, abiding season, or a fruitful season. Define your season and TRUST that you are never alone.

Daily Prayer:

Heavenly Daddy,

Oh Jesus, we may not understand why we have to go through different seasons in our lives, and sometimes that is the hardest part of it all, the why. Help me TRUST You as You prune, speak, and give fruit in my life. Help me seek and want You more than I want resolution and order in my life. Lift my head towards You and fill the spots of my heart that feel alone with Your presence. You are the I AM, You are the beginning and the end and everything in between. Help me trust in every season that You are defending, loving, and guiding my every step. I love you Jesus! In Jesus' name.

Love,

Your Daughter

Daily Jewels:

"I am the true vine, and my Father is the vinedresser. ² Every branch in me that does not bear fruit he takes away, and every branch that does bear fruit he prunes, that it may bear more fruit." John 15:1-2

"But you, O Lord, are a shield about me, my glory, and the lifter of my head." Psalm 3:3

"Whoever abides in me and I in him, he it is that bears much fruit, for apart from me you can do nothing." John 15:5

Daily Reflections:

_____

_____

_____

_____

_____

_____

_____

_____

_____

_____

_____

_____

_____

Don't forget your crown today!

Day 10: Diving Deep

Dive: plunge head first into water.

My boys love to swim. I'll never forget putting both of them in that little newborn raft and walking them into the water, praying they wouldn't scream their heads off. Mostly because all of our vacations were at the beach, and who wants to hear that on your vacation every year?

My oldest, Wilson, learned to swim around age 4, but he was deathly afraid of the deep end. He was a great swimmer, but there was something about his feet not being able to touch the floor that would make him absolutely lose it. Pure fear would come over him even thinking of jumping into the deep end. I would encourage him and even try to get in and let him latch onto me to show him that if he can swim in the shallow end, he can swim in the deep end. But he had already made up his mind that he would NEVER go into the deep end.

I can relate to Wilson in so many ways on this concept. I don't blame him for wanting to hang out in the shallow end where you feel comfortable. It has easy access to get out and grab a snack, and you can put down your feet to ease your mind that you aren't drowning. Nobody wants to feel like they are drowning. It's scary and has traumatic consequences.

As babies and even toddlers in our faith, it's ok to hang out in the shallow end to check things out and find our footing. But as we discover who Jesus is in our lives, we should slowly walk closer to the deep end or maybe even get out to jump in. Maybe that's you. You have committed your life to Jesus

Christ and you believe He is the Savior of the world, but you are staring at the deep end like it isn't for you. In Psalm 139 God tells us that He knew us when were under the Earth. It also goes on to say that we are "wonderfully made." If He created us so intimately and wonderfully, don't you think He wants us to experience ALL HE has for us? Sometimes we get so wrapped up in the fear of the unknown. We may wonder how it will feel when we jump. We may fear what people will think about us as our head goes under water.

When Wilson turned 6, he finally walked over to the diving board without even telling anyone, and JUMPED! Out of nowhere he had a blast of courage come over him, and he did it. The smile on his face when he surfaced showed me that it was worth it. But guess what? You can never experience that gift unless you jump. Our Heavenly Father has so many amazing things for our lives but sometimes we are too busy in the shallow end or too fearful to JUMP. Spend some time with God today and ask Him to help you discover where you have stayed comfortable. Allow your feet to slowly rise from the floor, hold your breath, and trust in the ONE who beautifully designed you. JUMP!

Daily Prayer:

Heavenly daddy,

Help me dive into the deep end with You. Give me YOUR courage to not worry about the "what ifs" or how it will feel or look if I dive right in. I want every blessing, gift, defeat, victory, and favor from YOU. I know You will be right there with me, giving me oxygen when I need it, and pulling me up when I feel like I am drowning. You created me for the deep end. Thank you Lord for not letting me settle. Here I go Jesus, I am ready for everything You have for me, let's jump together. In Jesus' name.

Love,

Your Daughter

>>>———————————<<<

Daily Jewels:

"Like newborn infants, long for the pure spiritual milk, that by it you may grow up into salvation— if indeed you have tasted that the Lord is good." 1 Peter 2:2-3

"For though by this time you ought to be teachers, you need someone to teach you again the basic principles of the oracles of God. You need milk, not solid food, for everyone who lives on milk is unskilled in the word of righteousness, since he is a child. But solid food is for the mature, for those who have their powers of discernment trained by constant practice to distinguish good from evil." Hebrews 5:12-14

"My frame was not hidden from you, when I was being made in secret, intricately woven in the depths of the earth. Your eyes saw my unformed substance; in your book were written, every one of them, the days that were formed for me; when as yet there was none of them." Psalm 139:15-16

Daily Reflections:

_____

_____

_____

_____

_____

_____

_____

_____

_____

_____

_____

_____

Don't forget your crown today!

Day 11: Charge Me Up

Battery Charger: a device for charging or recharging batteries.

The other day I woke up, put on my gym clothes (I actually worked out that day), and grabbed my phone. I noticed it was on 7%. Don't you just hate that? I rarely forget to plug my phone in before bed, and I was instantly annoyed because I had errands and calls to make. I knew my phone would die, and I wouldn't be as productive as I desired. I felt rushed most of the day. I noticed it was almost 1 am, and I still didn't have everything done. But you better believe that I didn't forget to plug my phone to charge before I crawled into bed. As I stuck the chord in and laid it down, I felt the Lord bring to remembrance the scripture, "Come to me all who are weary." It caught me off guard and then it hit like a punch in the face! I treated my phone better than myself. Stay with me here, because I truly feel like most of you will relate.

The phone has to be plugged into a device each night to "charge up." Well guess what ladies! We are the same way. We are so busy throughout the day saving the world one casserole at a time, or driving our kids to 457 places, or maybe with work or volunteering. We don't give ourselves the time we need to "recharge." There are many sources we can use to charge up, but remember that if you have an iPhone, you cannot use an Android charger. It has to be specific to that brand. As daughters of the King, there is only ONE source we need to plug our hearts and souls into, and that is our Lord and Savior, Jesus Christ.

There are temporary things that help us relax like a massage, pedicure, lunch with a friend, or a nap, but these things only last a short time. If you want to fill an empty void, or feel a love that conquers all, then that only comes from time with our Heavenly Daddy. Opening up the Word of God or praying is like a direct line of energy that will fill your soul and give your weary heart encouragement.

Every night we plug our phones in so that when we wake up it will be at 100% and ready for whatever we need (phone calls, texts, emails, Pinterest, Instagram, or Facebook). It's time we start fueling our souls for what our day brings (disappointments, conversations, exciting news, changes in our schedule, or victories). We may not "feel" 100% sure about our purpose in life, how well we are performing at work, or how much we are loved. But when we are plugged into the Source of Life none of that matters because God's Word reminds us that,

"And after you have suffered a little while, the God of all grace, who has called you to his eternal glory in Christ, will himself restore, confirm, strengthen, and establish you." 1 Peter 5:10

Daily Prayer:

Heavenly Daddy,

Some days I feel like I am functioning on 35% energy and using only some of the gifts You have given me. I am sorry that I look to outside sources to "recharge" me. Help remind me throughout the day that YOU are the only source that will give me strength and the ability to live and function at 100%. I cannot do anything without You Jesus, teach me to depend more on being led by the Holy Spirit instead of my own strength. In Jesus' name.

Love,

Your Daughter

Daily Jewels:

"For nothing will be impossible with God."

Luke 1:37

But He said, "The things that are impossible with people are possible with God."

Luke 18:27

"And after you have suffered a little while, the God of all grace, who has called you to his eternal glory in Christ, will himself restore, confirm, strengthen, and establish you." 1 Peter 5:10

Daily Reflections:

_____

_____

_____

_____

_____

_____

_____

_____

_____

_____

_____

_____

Don't forget your crown today!

Day 12: Don't Quit

Quit: to give up

We have the cutest Golden Doodle in the world named Wrigley (Go cubbies)! I have learned so many lessons from our people-loving, lazy, and beautiful doodle, but there is one that changed my perspective on fighting for my dreams. Wrigley is part poodle and part golden retriever so he has a "hunting" instinct. He loves chasing down squirrels. He started this hunt as a little puppy and 2 years later he has NEVER given up on his need to catch one.

One day I was trying to work in my office and I kept hearing Wrigley bark. It was driving me crazy, so I went outside and realized he was jumping up and down on this tree going wild. I started yelling, "Wrigley STOP, you cannot catch that squirrel, please stop." I stood there and watched him. I know he heard me, but my voice did not dictate his actions. He was determined to bark that thing down and eat it.

When the squirrel came down, the chase continued. I said a quick prayer that he would shut up so I could get some work done and slowly walked back inside. I sat down and realized that Wrigley was not just adorable, he wasn't a quitter. He was determined and focused. Regardless of how many days he pursued a squirrel, he never caught one. It didn't matter how much energy it took, or how loud the voice was that was yelling for him to stop. I stared down at my planner and realized that I had stopped writing and even stopped trying to fit it in my days. I felt discouraged and wondered why I wasn't motivated to finish this devotional. I was listening to a voice that seemed so loud and yelled, "nobody will read it!" I grew weary of distractions, and I knew right then that I needed to be more like my cute, willful, and energized Golden doodle.

He knew exactly what he wanted, and so did I! He woke up every morning ready to go, but most mornings I allowed 78 other tasks to take priority. He drowned out the voice of negativity, and I turned up the volume. My sweet sisters, it's time we stop quitting on our goals and start moving towards everything God has for us. My intention was to never quit writing, but you couldn't tell that based on my actions. I lost focus and negativity drowned out God's voice. I don't know what you are facing today, but I pray if there is a goal or dream you desire to accomplish then I pray you wake up and be ready to chase it relentlessly. Do not let other voices, how crazy your goal may sound, or how long it may take you dictate your actions. And never forget to enjoy the chase. I am sitting at our local coffee shop by the fire listening to friends chatter, keys hitting the keyboard, and music playing in the background. I am 100% ok if only one person picks up this book because I am truly in my happy place writing what is on my heart. Sometimes it's not about the destination and more about the in between, don't miss it.

I have to let you know that about 8 months after watching Wrigley trying to climb the tree to grab that squirrel, he delivered one right to our front door. He was so proud to show me that he finally got it. It only took him 2 years, but he didn't care. It was gross but I couldn't help be excited he succeeded. Don't quit on your dreams ladies, you may not feel like you can climb that tree or run another day but with Christ ANYTHING is possible. You are never alone.

Daily Prayer:

Heavenly Daddy,

You did not give us a spirit of fear, but You give us a renewed strength to accomplish everything You have for us. Jesus, I pray I don't miss it. Help me drown out the negative voices and only focus on the goal you have given me to accomplish. Give me endurance to never quit and encouragement to push through the adversity. I want to enjoy the in between, so show me the beauty in the fight that can only come from You. In Jesus' name.

Love,

Your Daughter

Daily Jewels:

"Do you not know that in a race all the runners run, but only one gets the prize? Run in such a way as to get the prize." 1 Corinthians 9:24

"Because you know that the testing of your faith produces perseverance." James 1:3

"For the Spirit God gave us does not make us timid, but gives us power, love and self-discipline." 2 Timothy 4:7

Daily Reflections:

_____

_____

_____

_____

_____

_____

_____

_____

_____

Don't forget your crown today!

Day 13: Growing Hurts

Growth: the process of increasing.

I started going to CrossFit Pistol Creek because this momma needed to get in shape. They launched this fun "healthy habits" challenge, which would help hold us accountable. Every day if you drink water, go to the gym, eat healthy etc. you get to check it off in their app. At the end of the six weeks, whoever has the most points will win. Well ladies, you know I am very competitive, but I am also very lazy (these 2 traits always have caused me problems). But the second this was launched I dove all in. This challenge meant I would have to work out 6 days a week. Now for me that is a lot of days. I am that "seasonal" work out person that goes for a few months then takes a few months off, can you relate? I'll see some results, but then I travel or kids get sick and it's hard to go back. So then I just have to "restart," it's kind of frustrating but I do it to myself.

After 2 weeks of this challenge, I realized I was just going to live sore. Every muscle hurt! My hair even hurt. I couldn't even dry my hair because my arms were too sore. The Lord has taught me so many things about my discipline through this, but one thing He keeps whispering to me is, GROWING HURTS. I am tearing down muscles to build them back up so I can be leaner and look better in my leggings (because let's be honest, that is all I wear). But what about my spiritual life, what about your spiritual life? I think we can all agree we want to grow (which means increase) spiritually, but are we showing up every day ready for everything God has for us? I don't mean reading your Bible and saying a prayer to check it off your list, I am talking about digging deep and surrendering everything to God.

It's the hard things, the relationship issues, kid melt downs, financial problems, or medical scares that allow us to put our FAITH in action and truly cause us to grow. It's the pruning seasons, lonely times, and desperate feeling to hear from God that gets us on our knees and IT HURTS. But oh sweet daughter of the King, it's during these times when you fully depend on Christ that you grow because you become more like your Heavenly Father. When Jesus walked this earth and was tempted by the enemy, or someone rejected Him, He quoted His Fathers Words. He knew exactly where His strength came from.

As women, it's easy to take control and stay in our comfort zones. But God wants us to cling to the Hem of His garment like it's our only lifeline. Growing may be painful, but it's also beautiful because we can use it to help others. There are so many hurting people out there that need to be reminded that through Christ they can overcome. Don't be "seasonal" in your spiritual growth but choose to be ready for some pain, love, and encouragement. Embrace everything God has for you today.

Daily Prayer:

Heavenly Daddy,

I want to grow into the woman You have called me to be, so help me when it's hard to lean on YOU. I know I will experience hurt and pain on earth. But I also know that You will give me peace and comfort and never leave me in the times I need you the most. Give me the discipline I need to show up with a willing heart to be obedient to everything You have for me. Increase my faith in YOU, Jesus even when it hurts. In Jesus' name.

Love,

Your Daughter

Daily Jewels:

"And a woman who had been suffering from a hemorrhage for twelve years, came up behind Him and touched the fringe of His cloak; for she was saying to herself, "If I only touch His garment, I will get well." But Jesus turning and seeing her said, "Daughter, take courage; your faith has made you well." At once the woman was made well." Matthew 9:20-22

"In this you greatly rejoice, even though now for a little while, if necessary, you have been distressed by various trials, so that the proof of your faith, being more precious than gold which is perishable, even though tested by fire, may be found to result in praise and glory and honor at the revelation of Jesus Christ." 1 Peter 1:6-7

"The apostles said to the Lord, "Increase our faith!" Luke 17:5

Daily Reflections:

_____

_____

_____

_____

_____

_____

_____

_____

_____

_____

_____

_____

Don't forget your crown today!

Day 14: Begin Again

Again: another time; once more.

Have you ever had to "restart" something? Think about it for a second. Maybe you had to start a new job after being at one for 25 years, or maybe you had to begin another relationship after one ended. If you are like me, you probably had to "restart" working out multiple times throughout the year. Starting over can be very difficult, and honestly it exhausts me to even think about the times I had to pick myself up from the floor to begin again. You know the feeling I am sure, where you feel like you worked so hard on something but then it just ended, and you are left alone wondering how in the world you could ever begin again.

It's a place we don't always look forward to, but we also know it's inevitable. You often hear quotes like "the comeback will be greater than the setback," or "your greatest victory is just never quitting." While that all sounds great it doesn't touch the feeling of failure you experience. Maybe you are going through this now or helping a friend up off the floor, and you just need some encouragement. Well, here it is.

GOD IS BIGGER THAN ANY SETBACK! He just is. After reading the book of John in the Bible and studying Jesus's ministry on the earth, I truly believe that our "setbacks," "rejections," or "failures" are part of His plan for our lives. If we didn't have these things, then how would we trust God more? I pray all of the time for God to give me opportunities to be His light out in the Word. The reality is that I can't be God's light if my life is perfect, and I don't experience the feeling of falling flat on my face. These things don't happen so that we can feel pain or frustration. They happen so we can feel the God of the universe so close to us and depend on Him to help us "begin again."

Our failures are God's opportunities to get close enough and build us back up. And this leads me to another great quote, "It's not about me." None of us want to look like a failure in front of other people, especially in the social media world. But when we live our life for a Kingdom purpose we realize that it's not about us anyway. So grab a hold of your crown, straighten it up a little and lift your head high because your confidence doesn't come from life "working out" how you planned, your confidence comes from the Lord!

Daily Prayer:

Heavenly Daddy,

I pray You give me the strength to get up and "begin again." I pray that I depend on You and not worry about what people think of me when I have to "begin again." Lord, guide me and surround me with people who will love me through this struggle. Help me be an encouragement to someone who may be experiencing this. Thank You, Jesus, for always being there when my face is flat on the ground.

In Jesus' name.

Love,

Your Daughter

Daily Jewels:

"But as for you, be strong and do not give up, for your work will be rewarded." 2 Chronicles 15:7

"Therefore humble yourselves under the mighty hand of God, that He may exalt you at the proper time.." 1 Peter 5:6

"I will not leave you as orphans; I will come to you." John 14:18

Daily Reflections:

_____

_____

_____

_____

_____

_____

_____

_____

Don't forget your crown today!

Day 15: Board of Directors:

Advisor: a person who gives advice in a particular field.

My sister, Keeli Boyce, is one of the smartest women I know. She is an entrepreneur and sits on multiple Boards in our small town. She loves serving in our community, and she has a true gift of fundraising for incredible causes. These organizations want her to sit on their board because they want her advice and opinion. They know she will add value to their cause, and it will help them accomplish their goals.

A few years ago, I realized that my "life" needed a board of directors. My love for people had allowed me to let so many people speak into my life and I kind of felt lost. Between social media and people's opinions of my job, ministry, and family, my head was spinning. I have always been a dreamer, but I almost felt like I was on a treadmill going NOWHERE. Can you relate?

I finally set some boundaries and created my own "Board of Directors." I needed to seek people who had the same value system as me and are enjoying the things I truly desire. I needed to find a mom who raised boys to be Godly men, and a leader who can lead with love. I also needed someone who is reaching their health goals, and a woman in ministry that continues to point others to Christ and Christ alone. As I prayed the Lord made it clear whom He wanted me to reach out to for mentorship. Today I have a tribe of women I allow to give me advice and speak life into me. I had to eliminate many voices that weren't adding value. I still love those people from a distance, however they aren't on my Board.

I want to encourage you to pray about who you are allowing to pour into you, and for you to create your own Board of directors. You should have women who leave you encouraged and adds value to the direction God is guiding you. Also, make sure they aren't just "yes" friends, but people who can correct you in love without putting you down.

We only have one life and since it isn't a dress rehearsal, I think we need to take our Board of Directors seriously. This also applies to who you "follow" on social media. Remember that what you see, hear, and put in your heart and mind is also what comes out. The unfollow button is a beautiful thing. If someone frustrates you or is negative, guess what, you don't have to see it. A few of the women on my Board don't even know it, but I follow them on social media because they speak truth and point me to Christ. I pray that you allow time in your schedule to seek out the right people to speak into your life; it matters!

Daily Prayer:

Heavenly Daddy,

Lord, I pray You place the right people in my life to advise me and give me the right counsel. I pray that I can set boundaries, and I can continue to grow in my relationship with You because I am surrounding myself with people who encourage me. I pray You send people for me to encourage. Thank You Jesus for your Word that tells us that "without counsel plans fail" (Proverbs 15:22). Help me be aware of who I am allowing to speak into my life. In Jesus' name.

Love,

Your Daughter

Daily Jewels:

"Without counsel plans fail, but with many advisers they succeed." Proverbs 15:22

"The way of the fool is right in his own eyes, but a wise man listens to advise." Proverbs 12:15

"The one who gets wisdom loves life; the one who cherishes understanding will soon prosper." Proverbs 19:8

Daily Reflections:

_____

_____

_____

_____

_____

_____

_____

_____

Don't forget your crown today!

Day 16: Whisper

Sound: Sound produced by continuous and regular vibrations, as opposed to noise.

When I looked up the definition of "sound," the last part caught my attention, "as opposed to noise." So many times in my life I have craved to hear God's voice, especially when I needed to make a big decision or just when feeling discouraged. Have you ever struggled with wondering what His voice sounds like? If you are like me, you wonder if it's your mind, His voice, or your mom speaking. I have prayed many times for God to make it clear to me if it's Him. Honestly I expected His voice to sound a little like Morgan Freeman's (low and strong). But scripture reminds us in 1 King's 19 that His voice is "still and small."

When someone starts to whisper, the automatic response is to come closer so you can hear what he or she is saying. I truly believe that is why God's voice doesn't sound like thunder, but it's more of a whisper. God wants to draw us so close that we not only hear His voice, we obey it. God's voice isn't just noise but a distinct sound that usually follows with a rush of Peace through your body knowing your Heavenly Father is speaking straight to you. Sometimes you can hear it when you are reading His Word, praying, or just being still.

I don't know what you are going through right now or why you need the calmness of His voice. But let me encourage you by reminding you that God is always speaking, and it's us who rarely listens. There are many voices swirling around our minds and through social media that we forget the ONE voice we crave and need. It is always there waiting for us to stop and listen. The creator of the Universe wants you to come closer to hear His words and encouragement. You will know His whisper because His words will fill the empty void in your soul. Today, dive into 1 Kings 19:9-18 and read how the Lord speaks to Elijah. This will show you how the Lord comforts Him with His whisper and instruction in a moment of discouragement. Your Heavenly Father is waiting for you, sweet daughter.

Daily Prayer:

Heavenly Daddy,

Thank You for drawing me closer to Your whisper. Help me discern Your voice above every noise out there. I pray that as I go throughout today and the rest of this week You help me through the Holy Spirit to know when it's You. Thank you for loving me so much that You never stop chasing after me. I pray against any distractions from Your voice. I pray I can continue to hear Your voice through prayer, reading Your Word, and sitting still. I love you, in Jesus' name.

Love,

Your Daughter

Daily Jewels:

"And after the earthquake a fire, but the Lord was not in the fire. And after the fire the sound of a low whisper." 1 Kings 19:12

"Now is my soul troubled. And what shall I say? 'Father, save me from this hour'? But for this purpose I have come to this hour. Father, glorify your name." Then a voice came from heaven: "I have glorified it, and I will glorify it again." John 12:27-28

"Call to me and I will answer you and tell you great and unsearchable things you do not know." Jeremiah 33:3

Daily Reflections:

_____

_____

_____

_____

_____

_____

_____

_____

Don't forget your crown today!

Day 17: Misunderstood

Misunderstood: incorrectly interpreted or understood.

Have you ever felt misunderstood? If you are married, a parent, or well a human being for that matter I know the answer is YES. It's impossible to go through life with relationships and avoid conflict without being misunderstood. It goes hand in hand with it. And if you are a control freak like me, you will try to "fix" the misunderstanding so everyone knows your true heart.

Whether you have experienced this in the past or currently dealing with it, I believe the enemy of the world uses this to steal our identity. When someone in your life misunderstands your words or decisions, you automatically feel like you have to "justify" your actions. And let's be honest, it hurts when someone you truly love doesn't give you grace or refuses to takes the time to "hear your heart." I have experienced this many times in my life, and the hardest part for me is knowing someone is thinking or talking negative about me because of the misunderstanding.

I want to encourage you today, whether you are being misunderstood or someone through a misunderstanding offends you, there is hope. When Jesus walked this Earth, He was on a mission to fulfill His destiny. He had people love Him, reject Him, and ignore Him but it NEVER affected His purpose. Rejection never defined Jesus, and it shouldn't define you either. God has a specific purpose for you TODAY regardless if someone else believes in it or not.

It doesn't matter if others celebrate you, make fun of you, or just don't understand because it's for you NOT them. Dive into the book of John and read how Jesus interacted with the ones who chose to not truly see who He was. You will quickly see a Savior that has His eyes so fixed on His Heavenly Father that it doesn't distract Him.

I don't know what your day holds. I don't know if you have any conflict, or how busy you are, but I do want to remind you that as a daughter of the King you only have one person in your life to be obedient to, and that is Jesus Christ. What you focus on grows and what you ignore dies so I pray today you focus on what God has for your life and nothing or nobody else. Your purpose matters too much to allow someone's misunderstanding to dictate how you feel or act. Don't give your Peace away to anyone. Your Heavenly Father has already gone before you and is always fighting for you; you just keep looking up.

Daily Prayer:

Heavenly Daddy,

Thank You for never rejecting me and always loving me in spite of me. Help me fix my eyes on YOU and Your purpose for my life. I pray Your light shines as I navigate through conflict and relationships. Help me to be an includer for others that may be experiencing being misunderstood. I want to point others to You. Thank You for being our example of how to love. In Jesus' name.

Love,

Your Daughter

>>>>———————————<<<

Daily Jewels:

"Let your eyes look directly forward, and your gaze be straight before you." Proverbs 4:25

"...looking to Jesus, the founder and perfector of our faith, who for the joy that was set before him endured the cross, despising the shame, and is seated at the right hand of the throne of God." Hebrews 12:2

Daily Reflections:

_____

_____

_____

_____

_____

Don't forget your crown today!

Day 18: Uniquely You

Unique: being the only one of its kind; unlike anything else.

What is one quality about your personality that you or other people might think is "unique?" If you are unsure of what I mean reread the definition above. What about your personality is one of a kind? We live in the world where we can point to a screen to analyze other people's lives and personalities in seconds, and it can sometimes make us feel less than. We live in the world where we are scared to be genuine because sometimes showing our uniqueness scares people away.

I want to challenge you to think differently. When God made you so perfectly in your mother's womb, he made sure you had uniqueness that only YOU held. That uniqueness includes the quirky, awkward, and funny things you often try to hide. Don't hide what God planted inside of you, sweet daughter. You were created in "His Image," and God doesn't make mistakes.

It's easy to want to "blend" into the crowd because it may keep you in the background. But sometimes making a habit of hiding can force us to shrink back the things God wants to use in our lives to make an impact. Life is too short to worry about what people think about our uniqueness; instead let's embrace it today. Don't apologize if you snort when you laugh, go ahead and force hug others, and enjoy the fact that God made you perfectly YOU. We are all different, made by our Creator, and perfected through Jesus's death and resurrection on the cross. Now let's start living awake, embracing every flaw, beauty, and mistake.

You are the only one that can live out YOUR destiny today. Do it by being uniquely YOU.

Daily Prayer:

Heavenly Daddy,

It's hard sometimes to look past the things that make me different. So I pray You help me live my life exactly the way You made me, because You made me perfectly. Help me to see other people's uniqueness's and encourage them to keep living their lives God has blessed them with. Help me to never shrink back and to always embrace everything You have created. Help me to see all of my personality traits through YOUR EYES. In Jesus' name.

Love,

Your Daughter

Daily Jewels:

"I knew you before I formed you in your mother's womb. Before you were born I set you apart and appointed you as my prophet to the nations." Jeremiah 1:4-5

"For we are his workmanship, created in Christ Jesus for good works, which God prepared beforehand, that we should walk in them." Ephesians 2:10

"Yet you, LORD, are our Father. We are the clay, you are the potter; we are all the work of your hand." Isaiah 64:8

Daily Reflections:

_____

_____

_____

_____

_____

_____

_____

_____

_____

Don't forget your crown today!

Day 19: Legacy

Legacy: Something handed down or received from an ancestor or predecessor.

Growing up I heard the word "legacy" often. My grandfather, Fred Loveday, would always remind us that everyone leaves a legacy, and it's up to us to make sure it lasts much longer than us. When I was younger, I didn't give that word much thought, but now after having two boys I know that legacy matters more than I ever dreamed. What does the word mean to you?

Some people believe that leaving a legacy means to make sure we are leaving a financial impact on our family. Some may think it means to leave your loved ones with material things. But I believe legacy is more nostalgic than that. I don't think we "leave" a legacy; I believe we "live" our legacy. And it starts every morning when we open our eyes. It's not something that just sits in our bank account; it's what we do, what we say, how we act, and how we react to others. It's what happens within our four walls when no one is looking. It's our integrity, morals, ethics, and actions.

Our loved ones, people on social media, our friends, and family are always watching and listening. We choose daily how we make others feel when we leave a room. This kind of legacy doesn't die when we do. If you love like Jesus and leave people feeling that they matter, then your legacy lingers for generations. That is what matters most.

I pray today you focus on what legacy you are leaving with others. I hope you are encouraged by the fact that as a daughter of the King you can leave an "eternal legacy" with everyone you meet by sharing Jesus's love and story. Now, go live your legacy and live it to the fullest. Leave a piece of you and the light of Jesus with everyone you come in contact with today.

Daily Prayer:

Heavenly Daddy,

Thank You for giving us an opportunity to have a, Kingdom legacy, we can share with everyone. I pray today that I can shine brighter, look people in the eyes, and let them know they matter. I pray I leave Your light and encouragement everywhere I walk, and that my legacy is built by loving others. I pray Your Loving Legacy is passed down to generations in my family, and people continue to see YOU in all I do. In Jesus' name.

Love,

Your Daughter

Daily Jewels:

"You shall love the Lord your God with all your heart and with all your soul and with all your might. And these words that I command you today shall be on your heart. You shall teach them diligently to your children, and shall talk of them when you sit in your house, and when you walk by the way, and when you lie down, and when you rise." Deuteronomy 6:5-7

"One generation shall commend your works to another, and shall declare your mighty acts." Psalm 145:4

Daily Reflections:

_____

_____

_____

_____

_____

_____

_____

_____

_____

Don't forget your crown today!

Day 20: Stronger

Strong: able to withstand great force or pressure.

Whether you are reading this in the morning, on your lunch break, or before bed I want to remind you how strong you are. YES YOU! You are so strong. You were created with a supernatural strength, which gives you the ability to OVERCOME any obstacle. If you are like me there are many days you don't feel very strong so I am here to tell you that your feelings lie to you. Seriously, I lie to myself all of the time. Last night, I told myself that I could eat 7 Oreos because my husband has been gone and I deserve them (why are Oreos so good)? Today, I told myself I didn't need to work out because I had already been 4 times this week. I AM A LIAR and I can probably guess you lie to yourself too. We have to stop believing everything we think and start talking back, because we are STRONG women who were created for greatness.

Have you ever pushed yourself to the limit at the gym or working long hours? You get fatigued or tired and your body or brain wants to stop. But you keep pushing and fighting. We have strength inside of us that our minds try to stop every single day. We have to be aware of the negativity that begins and create a new habit in our brains to remind us how we can overcome and reach our goal. God didn't create us to struggle. He created us to worship Him in spirit and truth. God didn't create us to stop when it got hard. The Bible says we can do all things through Christ (Philippians 4:13). He didn't say we could do all the things.

He created us to depend on Him. You see, we don't need to muster up the strength on our own, we just need to release control to our Savior. So take a deep breath, because you also weren't created to do it all on your own. Run into the arms of your Savior and open up the only Book that is ALIVE and allow yourself to lean on the solid ROCK. You are precious to your Heavenly Father, and He wants to give you His strength so you can face any obstacle with His strength. That is how much you are loved.

Daily Prayer:

Heavenly Daddy,

I need Your strength today Lord, I am tired. I am thankful I don't have to dig deep inside of me to muster up what I need to get through today. I can just depend on Your Word to help me fight. Your Word says that where I am weak, You are strong. THANK YOU for being my rock and allowing me to fall into Your arms. I don't have to be strong; I just need You because You are all that I need. In Jesus' name.

Love,

Your Daughter

Daily Jewels:

"On God my salvation and my glory rest; the rock of my strength, my refuge is in God." Psalm 62:7

"But the LORD has been my stronghold, And my God the rock of my refuge." Psalm 94:22

"Trust in the LORD forever, For in GOD the LORD, we have an everlasting Rock." Isaiah 26:4

Daily Reflections:

_____

_____

_____

_____

_____

_____

_____

Don't forget your crown today!

Day 21: Alive

Alive: having life: not dead or inanimate.

I don't know when you will pick up this book and read this particular day. You may be facing something difficult or maybe you are on the mountaintop enjoying life. Maybe it's just a normal "like every other day" moment. I just wanted to take a whole day to remind you how amazing you are. There are so many voices telling us who we are; social media makes it easy to compare, and sometimes our own minds can be our worst enemy. You may or may not have someone in your life reminding you that you were created for greatness. So regardless, I want to let you know that today God has a plan for you. This plan is for you to grow closer to HIM, your Heavenly Father. Don't you just love that? We don't have to strive or do for Him; we just have to be in His presence. So today, before you go throughout your day or before you go to bed spend some time with your Savior. Grab your Bible and turn to Ephesians 2 and let Him remind you are alive in Christ. Sometimes we need a reminder to wake up. Then I want you to shut your Bible and pray. Ask God what HE wants you to read. The Bible says in Hebrews that the words are SHARP and ALIVE, and God wants to show you something specific. Sometimes we just forget to ask.

I don't know about you but I want to feel ALIVE and HOPEFUL. I truly believe reading God's Word and praying to Him will remind you that your heartbeat has purpose. This isn't some cheesy "rah rah" session that has a short-term feeling of hope. This is a soul touching and a soul healing that can pierce your heart and mind forever. Your Heavenly Father is waiting for you today.

Heavenly Daddy,

I want to feel Your presence today. Speak to me and show me what Scripture You want to reveal to me. Help me be patient to wait for Your prompting or voice. I am sorry for not asking you more often and I pray that today you fill my soul with hope and show me how much you love me through your Word. So many people are living asleep to the fact that we are ALIVE in you. Wake me up to your wisdom. In Jesus' name!

Love,

Your Daughter

Daily Jewels:

"For the word of God is living and active, sharper than any two-edged sword, piercing to the division of soul and of spirit, of joints and of marrow, and discerning the thoughts and intentions of the heart." Hebrews 4:12

"For this reason it says, "Awake, sleeper, and arise from the dead, And Christ will shine on you." Ephesians 5:14

Daily Reflections:

_____

_____

_____

_____

_____

_____

_____

_____

_____

_____

_____

_____

_____

_____

Don't forget your crown today!

Day 22: Created to Move

Move: to go or pass to another place or in a certain direction with a continuous motion.

Have you ever had a trip planned that you just didn't feel prepared for? Maybe you are like me and you wait to pack until 45 minutes before you leave. Regardless, it can be stressful packing, trying finish up last minute work or chores, and then you have to fight through the security line (and then redress). There have been so many times that I plop in the seat at the gate with exhaustion even before the trip begins.

On a recent trip to the beautiful state of Arizona I had a similar experience. I was excited to finally get on the plane to close my eyes and rest. It took forever to board and then about the time we were supposed to taxi out the stewardess let us know that we were delayed due to something being broken in the bathroom. I looked around and some people seemed fine. But there were many that grabbed their phones to check their connection times or call their loved ones. The guy beside me seemed worried about how the rest of his travel day would end up. I said a little prayer in hopes it wouldn't take long. Fifteen minutes went by and we were told there was a delay due to weather. This is the moment frustration set in with everyone. You could feel it. I texted my husband, who is pilot, and he reassured me if I missed my connecting flight they would find another one. I was worried – and hot, why are airplanes so hot?

God taught me many things that day, but one thing that I believe will resonate with you is, "we were not created to sit idle." We all booked our flight purposefully to get to our desired destination. We planned, packed, and rushed to make it on time. The second we had to wait, panic started to settle in our hearts. I am sure some had to cancel business meetings and many missed their connections (I sprinted to mine and barely made it).

There is a reason for the frustration and that is because God created us to MOVE. When we were created in our mother's womb with our gifts and talents it was for a purpose and for a destination that only we can fulfill. The excitement you have when you walk on the beach the first time, the fresh air of hiking in the woods, the smell of a campfire, and the laughs of your family making memories are all part of our destination. Sometimes it isn't the end goal or the second we finally "make" it to where we are supposed to be that matters. It's about the process of growing closer to our Creator. We can trust that God has every step, word, and purpose planned and sealed. The only thing we need to do is move in HIS direction. There are so many things that are out of our control. But what we can control is our focus, attitude, and hearts toward God when our destination gets delayed or changed.

Don't miss the conversations in the chaos, the memories in the waiting, and the extraordinary in your ordinary daily routine. Jesus is always there with you, drawing you closer to Him. Ladies, let's MOVE towards that still small voice today and ask Him to show us what matters most.

Daily Prayer:

Heavenly Daddy,

Thank You for creating me with the excitement to move and the opportunity to experience You in the journey. I know You have a destination for me, but I pray that I can enjoy the small moments in the delay or ordinary. Help me make moves, have conversations, and seek You in everything. Give me the discernment to know which direction you want me to focus. Help me have a good attitude towards the changes in my life. I want to trust you more. Let's move Jesus, I am ready. In Jesus' name.

Love,

Your Daughter

Daily Jewels:

"Not that I have already obtained this or am already perfect, but I press on to make it my own, because Christ Jesus has made me his own. Brothers, I do not consider that I have made it my own. But one thing I do: forgetting what lies behind and straining forward to what lies ahead, I press on toward the goal for the prize of the upward call of God in Christ Jesus." Philippians 4:12-14

"I will instruct you and teach you in the way you should go; I will counsel you with my eye upon you." Psalm 32:8

"Let your eyes look directly forward, and your gaze be straight before you." Proverbs 4:25

Daily Reflections:

_____

_____

_____

_____

_____

_____

_____

_____

_____

Don't forget your crown today!

Day 23: Broken Pieces

Broken: violently separated into parts; damaged or altered by or as if by breaking.

Have you ever dropped glass and watched it shatter on the floor? It's the worst feeling. I have dropped casserole dishes, cups, and many plates trying to cook (and yes I do *try* to cook). It makes such a mess and has to be cleaned up very specifically so you don't cut the bottom of your feet or hands. And if you have small kids, it's even harder to make sure they don't come near the shattered glass so they don't get hurt.

Sometimes we go through things in life that make it feel like our hearts are being shattered. Have you ever wondered how God would put the pieces back together? Have you ever tried to put back shattered glass one by one? It's almost impossible to find every piece. So, you can forget trying to make into what it once was. My heart has been broken into pieces with tragedies in our family, rejection from friends, and facing the giants in my life. I have prayed many times and asked God to just "fix" it. I was tired of walking on the scattered glass and having to relearn lessons or being hurt by the sin of the world.

As women, we like things to be put back together. Naturally, we have the gift of nurturing things back to health. Sometimes God wants us to experience a shattered heart so He can make something NEW. We were never created to stay the same. Only through Jesus Christ can we experience the miracle of true transformation. Our Heavenly Father doesn't put us back together piece by piece. Instead, He will make a way when there is no way. He will shine light on the darkness. He will perform miracles that will mend and heal what was once broken.

Maybe you find yourself in a season where you feel your heart, emotions, or life is scattered, and you are scared to move because it will hurt. I want to remind you that you are not alone. Jesus walked this earth and experienced the same pain but he remained faithful to His Father. When His time came to be broken physically and die for our sin, it was in that moment our broken pieces stopped defining us and His grace filled the cracks. His love mends the wounds and His Word fills our souls with hope. He is giving us our breath back every time we bring our broken pieces to the cross. Sweet daughter, take a deep breath and feel your heartbeat. Know that the Holy Spirit is inside of you ready to transform the shattered pieces into a beautiful masterpiece. You are never alone.

Daily Prayer:

Heavenly Daddy,

I pray the shattered pieces of my life stop defining who I am. I pray that every single time I feel my lungs take a breath I am reminded that You are mending my brokenness into something that will give You Glory. Break my chains of feeling shattered and make me whole again. Thank You for dying on the cross for my sin and filling my life with grace. Thank you for always being faithful and for being the one person I can always go to in my brokenness. In Jesus' name.

Love,

Your Daughter

Daily Jewels:

"The LORD is near to the brokenhearted and saves those who are crushed in spirit." Psalm 34:18

"He heals the brokenhearted and binds up their wounds." Psalm 147:3

"The Spirit of the Lord GOD is upon me, Because the LORD has anointed me To bring good news to the afflicted; He has sent me to bind up the brokenhearted, To proclaim liberty to captives And freedom to prisoners;" Isaiah 61:1

Daily Reflections:

_____

_____

_____

_____

_____

_____

_____

_____

_____

Don't forget your crown today

Day 24: Setting Boundaries

Boundary: a line that marks the limits of an area; a dividing line.

When was the last time you left your door unlocked at night? Growing up, I am not even sure we would lock our doors. That was in the 80's and 90's but we live in a very different world now. A few weeks ago my husband was traveling and around 2 am I realized that I never shut the garage. I got that sick feeling in my stomach and sprinted to shut it before something bad happened. It took me forever to go back to sleep because I kept thinking of what "could have" happened. I think I have watched too many Lifetime movies over the years.

You know that feeling right? It's a vulnerable and insecure feeling that gets your heart rate up in seconds. I know there are trusting people out there who may not stress the way I do. But I can guarantee you that they aren't opening their door screaming for people to come in and steal their valuables. They aren't inviting anyone to dump their trash in the living room to hang out all hours of the night. Who in the world would do that?

As women we have allowed something just as bad happen in our minds. We allow people to walk into our lives and dump their toxic negativity into our hearts and minds. I have a "people pleaser" personality and I can't tell you how many years I allowed people to walk right into my life and treat me any way they wanted. I would protect my home every night, but during the day I chose not to protect my own heart and mind.

Don't allow people to walk right into your life and be negative. It's important to set healthy boundaries. I used to call "everyone" my best friend because I truly do love people (remember I force hug everyone). But the older I get the more I realize that other people's negativity ends up leaving a trashy smell everywhere I walk. I began to believe the lies and felt unworthy. I left the door wide open for my heart to be trampled on. Setting boundaries is important as you grow closer to the Lord because you need to know what is truth and what is healthy for you. You can love everyone, but some people you need to love from a distance. Not everyone wants the best for you and that is ok. You can love and pray for those people every day. You do not have to keep the doors open for just anyone to walk in and distort who you are. The louder God's voice is the easier it's to recognize which voice is encouraging and pointing you to Christ and which voice is dumping trash (lies) over the truth. Have discernment today on what you watch and listen to. Protect your minds and hearts and remember that Jesus had many followers, a dozen disciples, but he only had a few He called His "inner tribe." There is not a better example to follow than our own personal Savior. Allow God to heal any wounds or bitterness and know that having boundaries will protect what God created.....YOU!

Daily Prayer:

Heavenly Daddy,

Thank You for showing us how to set boundaries when You walked this Earth. You had followers that loved You, hated You, and even disciples who rejected You. You remained faithful to your Father and knew His Words would keep You focused on Him. Help me do that today and every day. Give me Your discernment with my relationships and give me the strength to set healthy boundaries in my life. In Jesus' name.

Love,

Your Daughter

Daily Jewels:

"When He set for the sea its boundary, so that the water would not transgress His command, When He marked out the foundations of the earth;" Proverbs 8:29

"One who has unreliable friends soon comes to ruin, but there is a friend who sticks closer than a brother." Proverbs 18:24

"Above all else, guard your heart, for everything you do flows from it." Proverbs 4:23

Daily Reflections:

_____

_____

_____

_____

_____

_____

_____

_____

_____

_____

_____

_____

_____

_____

Don't forget your crown today!

Day 25: Invisible Battles

Battle: fight or struggle tenaciously to achieve or resist something.

The other day I was walking around the mall and I started to people watch. Every season of life was represented, and I am sure they all had different errands and things they needed to purchase that day. There were many moms with toddlers, middle-aged men that looked like they were on their lunch break, and even teenagers hanging out (this was spring break time).

I was about to get up when I felt God whisper the words "watch the invisible battle." I sat back down and silently prayed and asked God what that meant. I looked around again, but this time people looked different. I saw the exhaustion in one mother's eyes. I saw the stress in a man who was clearly in a rush. I noticed the joy on a young girls face as she laughed with her friend. Regardless of their expression, I knew they were dealing with an "invisible battle." God was revealing to me that everyone has giants they face that only HE knows about.

I began to wonder what people thought of me that day. I had a smile on my face that covered up the insecurity I felt. I was exhausted and burdened. Nobody knew I was balancing a traveling husband, a job, a ministry, laundry, and everything in between. I felt the weight of the world on my shoulders that day, but the smile on my face showed strength I didn't feel inside. That day made me realize that giving extra kindness to people matters. We may not see people's battles, but we can give extra grace knowing that can help. A smile, an extra thank you, encouraging text, or a warm hug could be the Jesus someone needs that day.

 You may be facing a battle that looks invisible to everyone else, but always remember that God is fighting for you. He will bring people to encourage you, Scriptures to comfort you, and a love that pursues you. As you go throughout your day today ask God to give you His eyes. Ask for knowledge to recognize the person who has a bad attitude or seems frustrated. They may be fighting their "invisible battle" without the knowledge of our Savior. Be open to share your story and our Saviors love with them and give them an extra smile. There is nothing more beautiful than giving someone extra kindness and grace. Jesus does this for us every single day.

Daily Prayer:

Heavenly Daddy,

Lord, thank You for reminding me that everyone faces invisible battles that You only see. I pray You give me Your eyes and the wisdom to give extra grace and kindness. Help me remember that You are always there for us fighting our battles. Give me someone to encourage today. I pray I can share my story and faith and that I can keep a Kingdom focus on all of my conversations. In Jesus' name.

Love,

Your Daughter

Daily Jewels:

"The Lord will fight for you; you need only to be still." Exodus 14:14

"The horse is made ready for the day of battle, but victory rests with the Lord." Proverbs 21:31

"You are from God, little children, and have overcome them; because greater is He who is in you than he who is in the world." 1 John 4:4

"But thanks be to God, who gives us the victory through our Lord Jesus Christ." 1 Corinthians 15:57

Daily Reflections:

_____

_____

_____

_____

_____

_____

_____

_____

_____

_____

_____

_____

_____

_____

_____

_____

_____

_____

Don't forget your crown today!

Day 26: Audience of ONE

Audience: the assembled spectators or listeners at a public event, such as a play, movie, concert, or meeting.

How do you live for an audience of ONE when there are always hundreds watching? We live in the social media age where we have instant access and validation. If we have a problem, question, or an accomplishment we can gather likes and comments in seconds. And let's all be honest, it feels good to know people are cheering us on and supporting our families. I think we crave this kind of audience because all we have to do is sit behind a screen to gather answers and support quickly. I have been guilty of seeking out what other people think before I go to Jesus Christ. There are many incredible things about social media; my whole ministry began on Facebook, but I also believe the enemy can use it to distract us.

I live in East TN, so when our men's basketball team (Go Vols) started climbing to the top local TV stations started interviewing them. There are so many videos of them reminding everyone that they are a team of Faith and they play for an audience of ONE. Those 3 words have resonated in my heart. God has taken me on a journey of asking the simple question, "who am I living for?" Thankfully, I don't have to perform in front of thousands and try to bring a team to victory, but I do have a responsibility to live out the purpose God has for me. I have 2 little boys that watch every step I take and hear every word I speak. But I also have friends and family watching me through my "highlight reel" on social media. It can be a lot of pressure to make sure we look a certain way. I used to feel the need to show that we had successful businesses, a loving marriage, and a thriving ministry. But God has pruned and stripped me of so much selfishness and unhealthy validation. He has also reminded me that I don't have to perform, strive, or climb any ladder for His attention. He just loves me, because He loves me. Whew! How good does that feel to know that?

Before I post on social media, I always ask myself "why" am I posting this? Am I encouraging my audience, sharing a glimpse into our life, or am I seeking celebration and validation? These questions have helped me stay focused on keeping Christ the only eyes and ears I seek. I love social media and I think it's used for many great things. But I pray today that you are reminded which audience matters most. It feels good to get likes and comments but the feeling you get from your Heavenly Father when you are on your knees will change you forever. Sometimes, it's the invisible things that nobody sees that will transform you from the inside and people will eventually see it on the outside.

Never forget that you were created for God; not for success or other people. The only thing God wants from you is your attention.

Whether you are working, parenting, or serving you can live as if there is only ONE person watching, Jesus Christ. This mindset and heart shift will help you live with excellence with no pressure to seek validation from other people. When you can be successful or make mistakes without the worry about what other people think is when you start to live with a Holy confidence. Today, go live with an AUDIENCE OF ONE.

Daily Prayer:

Heavenly Father,

I pray that You help remind me when I need to seek you before anyone else. Help me try to eliminate other people's opinions or validation so I can focus on what YOU have for me. Fix my eyes on YOU and you alone. Search my heart; help me figure out if there are areas in my life where I am seeking others before you. Give me the strength to put my faith in action. In Jesus' name.

Love,

Your Daughter

Daily Jewels:

"Search me, O God, and know my heart; test me and know my anxious thoughts." Psalm 139:23

"Nothing in all creation is hidden from God. Everything is naked and exposed before his eyes, and he is the one to whom we are accountable." Hebrews 4:13

Daily Reflections:

_____

_____

_____

_____

_____

_____

_____

_____

_____

_____

_____

_____

_____

Don't forget your crown today!

Day 27: Jumping for Joy

Joy: a feeling of great pleasure and happiness; rejoice.

Have you ever met someone that was always full of joy? If you can think of that person, I want you to send them a text right now and thank them. Having a friend that is joyful is a true gift. I am sure the person you are thinking of (and maybe it's even you) is always smiling and people are naturally drawn to them. There are many happy people in the world, but a joyful person creates a different environment.

Joy is very different than happiness. Typically, happiness occurs when something great happens. What makes you happy? I love spending time with my family, working out with my tribe, and watching my boys play sports. Happiness is wonderful but it's also based on emotion. So when there is change, like my boys lose a game or my husband travels, the happiness can fade. Happiness fluctuates based on our circumstance.

Joy is deeper than a feeling, and it's also a choice. It's also a fruit of the Spirit. There are many things in life that can have our emotions scattered, but when you experience true joy you never want it to leave. I have learned that joy can only come from the Lord. One of my favorite attributes of our Heavenly Father is that He doesn't sleep and He has already gone before us. So when we experience things that don't make us "feel" good, we can choose if we are going to lean on Him for joy or allow our emotions to take over. Everybody has the potential to hurt us because we are all flesh. But Jesus will never leave or forsake us. You will be disappointed more when you seek external things or people to make you happy.

When you posture yourself towards Christ, you can have joy in the midst of any storm.

The world screams at us to chase happiness but God wants you to stop and give Him your attention. I truly believe we were all created with a void in our hearts that only He can fill. We can try to fill it with things that will make us happy temporarily but there is way more to life than a feeling. It's the eternal joy knowing you are protected and loved as a daughter of the King. God chose you, He wants you, and He loves you. He is your true joy. Remember, when the whole world changes, He remains the same. I pray today you see Gods joy in everything you face.

Daily Prayer:

Heavenly Daddy,

Thank You for being a Heavenly Father that never changes. You are the same yesterday, today, and forever. I am thankful I can find JOY in You regardless of my circumstance. Help me find joy in all things so Your light will shine through me. When I lay my head down at night to rest I can rest in knowing You are always loving and fighting for me. Thank you for being the only constant in my life. In Jesus' name.

Love,

Your Daughter

Daily Jewels:

"Jesus Christ is the same yesterday and today and forever." Hebrews 13:8

"For his anger is but for a moment, and his favor is for a lifetime. Weeping may tarry for the night, but joy comes with the morning." Psalm 30:5

"So also you have sorrow now, but I will see you again, and your hearts will rejoice, and no one will take your joy from you." John 16:22

Daily Reflections:

_____

_____

_____

_____

_____

_____

_____

_____

_____

Don't forget your crown today!

Day 28: Take a Risk

Risk taker: a person who takes risks.

If you know anything about my personality you know I love to take risks. My husband calls me a "free spirit," and says I am like a balloon in the clouds and he is holding onto the string. You are either like me or you are organized and like to have a plan. When we go on vacation, I love having no plan but my husband always has his "Danny Tanner clipboard of fun." Can you tell I grew up in the 90's?

Typically, you are either a planner or more of a free spirit. Are you the person who writes down what you do to mark it off your list? Or the person that can't because they lost the list? Regardless, I want to encourage you today to take a risk. Taking a risk and doing something outside of our comfort zones can be easier for some and almost impossible for others. The reason I want to take a whole day to remind you of the importance of taking a risk is because we weren't created to live for comfort. I believe God put so many amazing ideas inside of us, but fear keeps us from being obedient. I come across so many women who want to write a book, start a blog, or run their own business, but they are afraid to start. What if we were more afraid of being disobedient than failing? I can look back at my life and be reminded of the risks I failed at and the ones that were successful. In both circumstances I learned incredible lessons, grew as a person, and showed my boys that I am not afraid to do something different. So, what if you started a blog and only 30 people read it. What if you changed just one person's life with your story? Is it worth it? Life is too short to NOT take risks. Today I want you to pray and ask God if there is something you need to do, say, or start that you have been putting off.

There are probably one million devotions written and published, but that didn't stop me from sharing the message God has put on my heart. Remember to know what voice to listen to and what voice to ignore. You have everything you need inside of you because the Holy Spirit is there as your "helper." Fear doesn't have the Holy Spirit, but WE DO. We don't have to "feel" courageous to be, we don't have to know all the answers to start, we just have to take the risk and trust in the One who beautifully designed us.

Daily Prayer:

Heavenly Daddy,

I come to You and ask You to reveal anything I need to do that I am not being obedient about. Help show me the risks you want me to take, even if it scares me. Help me to put Your will before the fear I feel. Thank you for the comfort of knowing that if I put myself out there I am never alone.

Love,

Your Daughter

Daily Jewels:

"But the Helper, the Holy Spirit, whom the Father will send in my name, he will teach you all things and bring to your remembrance all that I have said to you." John 14:26

"Peace I leave with you; my peace I give to you. Not as the world gives do I give to you. Let not your hearts be troubled, neither let them be afraid." John 14:27

.."for God gave us a spirit not of fear but of power and love and self-control." 2 Timothy 1:7

Daily Reflections:

_____

_____

_____

_____

_____

_____

_____

_____

_____

Don't forget your crown today!

Day 29: Freedom

Freedom: the state of not being imprisoned or enslaved.

I love the definition of freedom. There is something so empowering when you know that you are NOT being imprisoned or enslaved. If you have accepted Jesus Christ as your personal Savior you know what it feels like to be free. When Jesus died on the Cross-, not only did He die but so did our past mistakes and sin. Jesus died to save us from ourselves. We were all born into our sinful nature (thanks Adam and Eve). We are all naturally selfish and full of pride, but Jesus changed everything. Our freedom begins the day we recognize that our Savior died and was raised 3 days later. He is alive and paid the ultimate price for us to be free.

Are you living free? You may feel imprisoned by your past or fear. You may feel trapped in a room with the door wide open, but you are scared to move. I believe so many women are bound by negative self-talk and comparison and are choosing to stay enslaved. Ladies, you are FREE and FORGIVEN. God's Word says in Isaiah 53:5

"But he was pierced for our transgressions, he was crushed for our iniquities; the punishment that brought us peace was on him, and by his wounds we are healed."

After Jesus was raised from the dead, He visited His disciples to show them that He was alive. One of the disciples, Thomas, didn't believe it until Jesus showed him his scars. It says in John 20:27

"Then he said to Thomas, "Put your finger here; see my hands.

Reach out your hand and put it into my side. Stop doubting and believe." Can you relate to Thomas? Maybe you have believed in Jesus a long time but like Thomas, your doubt and fear has kept you in bondage. You may have scars and hurts that have caused chains to bind and imprison you. Maybe you live in the world of comparison or you are in an identity crisis. What is holding you back from living in God's freedom for your life?

My prayer is that TODAY you would release it all to Jesus and believe that you are made NEW through Him. Jesus has already paid the price for you. Your hurts, past mistakes, and pain are already nailed to that cross. All you have to do accept this free gift of Grace and allow the Holy Spirit to remind you of WHO you are, DAUGHTER OF THE KING.

Daily Prayer:

Heavenly Daddy,

I AM FREE! Thank You for saving me from my own selfishness and my past hurts. I know you can save me from my current pain. Lord, help me BELIEVE and live HEALED. Break every chain, Jesus. Help me continue to lay everything at Your cross. Heal me from the inside out. Help me walk out of the prison that has kept me in bondage and walk straight into your arms, Jesus.

Love,

Your Daughter

Daily Jewels:

"Then he said to Thomas, "Put your finger here; see my hands. Reach   out your hand and put it into my side. Stop doubting and believe." John 20:27

"But he was pierced for our transgressions, he was crushed for our iniquities; the punishment that brought us peace was on him, and by his wounds we are healed." Isaiah 53:5

"And I am sure of this, that he who began a good work in you will bring it to completion at the day of Jesus Christ." Philippians 1:6

Daily Reflections:

_____

_____

_____

_____

_____

_____

_____

_____

_____

Don't forget your crown today!

Day 30: Daughter

Blessing: God's favor and protection.

I don't know what day you will be reading this, but wherever you are I hope it's beautiful and sunny. I am not sure what you will face today, a long day of work, running errands with little kids, or maybe you are retired and enjoying lunch with a friend. The last 30 days I pray you have been reminded of Gods unconditional love for you.

Today I want to remind you of one of His promises He has for you as His daughter.

"When you pass through the waters, I will be with you; and when you pass through the rivers, they will not sweep over you. When you walk through the fire, you will not be burned; the flames will not set you ablaze." Isaiah 43:2

You, my beautiful daughter, have Gods protection on your life. This does not mean that you won't experience pain or go through hard times. It means that those things won't overwhelm you when you are in the presence of your Heavenly Father who is always with you.

I pray that you pick up this jewel and place it in the center of your crown. This jewel reminds you of the power He has over your life and the promise that you are always in His hands. So, grab it, believe it, and cling to it. I hope you have learned the last 30 days that as your Father, He may have to set boundaries, help train you up, and push you out of your comfort zone, but He will ALWAYS be with you. He is your jewel, He is the extraordinary in your ordinary, and He is your hope.

You can walk into this day with confidence regardless of

your circumstances because you are a Daughter of the King. You belong to the one who breathed the Universe into existence. You were created with purpose, greatness, and love. So, now wake up and LIVE like it every single day. He has a Kingdom destiny placed on your life. He is your destiny and His love is your purpose. He wants you to share it with everyone you meet. There is nothing that matters more than sharing the extraordinary story of a Savior who died for us and rose again so that our sins could be forgiven. When we accept this free gift of grace and share it, we are living our purpose. Let's pass this jewel on today and share His amazing love so more people can live their eternal destiny.

Daily Prayer:

Heavenly Daddy,

Thank You Jesus for being my extraordinary jewel that shines bright. I pray that I have an opportunity to share about the sacrifice you made, and I can pass the gift of Grace on. I pray that people see You when they look at me. I pray every day I can grow closer and closer to You. Continue to remind me of all of Your promises You have on my life. I pray I live loved, healed, and victorious because I am a Daughter of the King, because that is who You say I am. In Jesus name.

Love,

Your Daughter

Daily Jewels:

"When you pass through the waters, I will be with you; and when you pass through the rivers, they will not sweep over you. When you walk through the fire, you will not be burned; the flames will not set you ablaze." Isaiah 43:2

"See what great love the Father has lavished on us, that we should be called children of God! And that is what we are!" 1 John 3:1

"She is clothed with strength and dignity, and she laughs without fear of the future." Proverbs 31:25

Daily Reflections:

_____

_____

_____

_____

_____

_____

_____

_____

Don't forget share your crown today!

Daily Jewels Index:

Brave Enough

"Be strong and courageous, and do the work. Do not be afraid or be discouraged for the LORD God, my God, is with you." 1 Chronicles 28:20

"Finally, be strong in the Lord and in his mighty power." Ephesians 6:10

"Be strong and let your heart take courage, all you who hope in the LORD." Psalm 31:24

Guiltless Nap

"Come to me, all you who are weary and burdened, and I will give you rest. Take my yoke upon you and learn from me, for I am gentle and humble in heart, and you will find rest for your souls." Mathew 11:28-29

"Do not be anxious about anything, but in every situation, by prayer and petition, with thanksgiving, present your requests to God. And the peace of God, which transcends all understanding, will guard your hearts and your minds in Christ Jesus." Philippians 4:6-7

Stop Screaming at Me

"For you are my rock and my fortress; For Your name's sake you will lead me and guide me." Psalm 31:33

"Make me walk in the path of your commandments, for I delight in it." Psalm 119:35

"Teach me to do your will, for you are my God; Let Your good Spirit lead me on level ground." Psalm 143:10

Love me, Love me Not

"Keep your life free from love of money, and be content with what you have, for he has said, "I will never leave you nor forsake you." Hebrews 13:5

"but God shows his love for us in that while we were still sinners, Christ died for us." Romans 5:8

"For am I now seeking the approval of man, or of God? Or am I trying to please man? If I were still trying to please man, I would not be a servant of Christ." Galatians 1:10

Dress Rehearsal

"Why, you do not even know what will happen tomorrow. What is your life? You are a mist that appears for a little while and then vanishes." James 4:14

"And I am sure of this, that he who began a good work in you will bring it to completion at the day of Jesus Christ." Philippians 1:6

"Wait for the Lord; be strong, and let your heart take courage; wait for the Lord!" Psalm 27:14

The Dreaded Mirror

"For you created my inmost being;

you knit me together in my mother's womb.

I praise you because I am fearfully and wonderfully made;

your works are wonderful,

I know that full well." Psalm 139:13-14

"For the Lord will be your confidence and will keep your foot from being caught." Proverbs 3:26

Don't Grow Weary

"So let us come boldly to the throne of our gracious God. There we will receive his mercy, and we will find grace to help us when we need it most." Hebrews 4:16

"Cast all your anxiety on Him because he cares for you." 1 Peter 5:7

"Look to the Lord and his strength; seek his face always." Psalm 105:4

"But he said to me, 'My grace is sufficient for you, for my power is made perfect in weakness.' Therefore I will boast all the more gladly of my weaknesses, so that the power of Christ may rest on me." 2 Corinthians 12:9

Help my Unbelief

"If you can! All things are possible for one who believes." Immediately the father of the child cried out and said, "I believe; help my unbelief!" Mark 9:23-25

"And he said to them, "Why are you afraid, O you of little faith?" Then he rose and rebuked the winds and the sea, and there was a great calm." Matthew 8:26

He said to them, "Because of your little faith. For truly, I say to you, if you have faith like a grain of mustard seed, you will say to this mountain, 'Move from here to there,' and it will move, and nothing will be impossible for you." Matthew 17:20

Pruning

"I am the true vine, and my Father is the vinedresser. [2] Every branch in me that does not bear fruit he takes away, and every branch that does bear fruit he prunes, that it may bear more fruit." John 15:1-2

"But you, O Lord, are a shield about me, my glory, and the lifter of my head." Psalm 3:3

"Whoever abides in me and I in him, he it is that bears much fruit, for apart from me you can do nothing." John 15:5

Diving Deep

"Like newborn infants, long for the pure spiritual milk, that by it you may grow up into salvation— if indeed you have tasted that the Lord is good." 1 Peter 2:2-3

"For though by this time you ought to be teachers, you need someone to teach you again the basic principles of the oracles of God. You need milk, not solid food, for everyone who lives on milk is unskilled in the word of righteousness, since he is a child. But solid food is for the mature, for those who have their powers of discernment trained by constant practice to distinguish good from evil." Hebrews 5:12-14

"My frame was not hidden from you, when I was being made in secret, intricately woven in the depths of the earth. Your eyes saw my unformed substance; in your book were written, every one of them, the days that were formed for me; when as yet there was none of them." Psalm 139:15-16

Charge me up

"For nothing will be impossible with God."

Luke 1:37

But He said, "The things that are impossible with people are possible with God."

Luke 18:27

"And after you have suffered a little while, the God of all grace, who has called you to his eternal glory in Christ, will himself restore, confirm, strengthen, and establish you." 1 Pet. 5:10

Don't Quit

"Do you not know that in a race all the runners run, but only one gets the prize? Run in such a way as to get the prize."

1 Corinthians 9:24

"Because you know that the testing of your faith produces perseverance."

James 1:3

"For the Spirit God gave us does not make us timid, but gives us power, love and self-discipline."

2 Timothy 4:7

Growing Hurts

"And a woman who had been suffering from a hemorrhage for twelve years, came up behind Him and touched the fringe of His cloak; for she was saying to herself, "If I only touch His garment, I will get well." But Jesus turning and seeing her said, "Daughter, take courage; your faith has made you well." At once the woman was made well." Matthew 9:20-22

"In this you greatly rejoice, even though now for a little while, if necessary, you have been distressed by various trials, so that the proof of your faith, being more precious than gold which is perishable, even though tested by fire, may be found to result in praise and glory and honor at the revelation of Jesus Christ." 1 Peter 1:6-7

"The apostles said to the Lord, "Increase our faith!" Luke 17:5

Begin Again

"But as for you, be strong and do not give up, for your work will be rewarded." 2 Chronicles 15:7

"Therefore humble yourselves under the mighty hand of God, that He may exalt you at the proper time.." 1 Peter 5:6

"I will not leave you as orphans; I will come to you." John 14:18

Board of Directors

"Without counsel plans fail, but with many advisers they succeed." Proverbs 15:22

"The way of the fool is right in his own eyes, but a wise man listens to advise." Proverbs 12:15

"The one who gets wisdom loves life; the one who cherishes understanding will soon prosper." Proverbs 19:8

Whisper

"And after the earthquake a fire, but the Lord was not in the fire. And after the fire the sound of a low whisper." 1 Kings 19:12

"Now is my soul troubled. And what shall I say? 'Father, save me from this hour'? But for this purpose I have come to this hour. Father, glorify your name." Then a voice came from heaven: "I have glorified it, and I will glorify it again." John 12:27-28

"Call to me and I will answer you and tell you great and unsearchable things you do not know." Jeremiah 33:3

Misunderstood

"Let your eyes look directly forward, and your gaze be straight before you." Proverbs 4:25

"...looking to Jesus, the founder and perfector of our faith, who for the joy that was set before him endured the cross, despising the shame, and is seated at the right hand of the throne of God." Hebrews 12:2

Uniquely You

"I knew you before I formed you in your mother's womb. Before you were born I set you apart and appointed you as my prophet to the nations." Jeremiah 1:4-5

"For we are his workmanship, created in Christ Jesus for good works, which God prepared beforehand, that we should walk in them." Ephesians 2:10

"Yet you, LORD, are our Father. We are the clay, you are the potter; we are all the work of your hand." Isaiah 64:8

Legacy

"You shall love the Lord your God with all your heart and with all your soul and with all your might. And these words that I command you today shall be on your heart. You shall teach them diligently to your children, and shall talk of them when you sit in your house, and when you walk by the way, and when you lie down, and when you rise." Deuteronomy 6:5-7

"One generation shall commend your works to another, and shall declare your mighty acts." Psalm 145:4

Stronger

"On God my salvation and my glory rest; the rock of my strength, my refuge is in God." Psalm 62:7

"But the LORD has been my stronghold, And my God the rock of my refuge." Psalm 94:22

"Trust in the LORD forever, For in GOD the LORD, we have an everlasting Rock." Isaiah 26:4

Alive

"For the word of God is living and active, sharper than any two-edged sword, piercing to the division of soul and of spirit, of joints and of marrow, and discerning the thoughts and intentions of the heart." Hebrews 4:12

"For this reason it says, "Awake, sleeper, and arise from the dead, And Christ will shine on you." Ephesians 5:14

Created to Move

"Not that I have already obtained this or am already perfect, but I press on to make it my own, because Christ Jesus has made me his own. Brothers, I do not consider that I have made it my own. But one thing I do: forgetting what lies behind and straining forward to what lies ahead, I press on toward the goal for the prize of the upward call of God in Christ Jesus." Philippians 4:12-14

"I will instruct you and teach you in the way you should go; I will counsel you with my eye upon you." Psalm 32:8

"Let your eyes look directly forward, and your gaze be straight before you." Proverbs 4:25

Broken Pieces

"The LORD is near to the brokenhearted and saves those who are crushed in spirit." Psalm 34:18

"He heals the brokenhearted and binds up their wounds."

Psalm 147:3

"The Spirit of the Lord GOD is upon me, Because the LORD has anointed me To bring good news to the afflicted; He has sent me to bind up the brokenhearted, To proclaim liberty to captives And freedom to prisoners;" Isaiah 61:1

Setting Boundaries

"When He set for the sea its boundary, so that the water would not transgress His command, When He marked out the foundations of the earth;" Proverbs 8:29

"One who has unreliable friends soon comes to ruin, but there is a friend who sticks closer than a brother." Proverbs 18:24

"Above all else, guard your heart, for everything you do flows from it." Proverbs 4:23

Invisible Battles

"The Lord will fight for you; you need only to be still." Exodus 14:14

"The horse is made ready for the day of battle, but victory rests with the Lord." Proverbs 21:31

"You are from God, little children, and have overcome them; because greater is He who is in you than he who is in the world." 1 John 4:4

"But thanks be to God, who gives us the victory through our Lord Jesus Christ." 1 Corinthians 15:57

Audience of ONE

"Search me, O God, and know my heart; test me and know my anxious thoughts." Psalm 139:23

"Nothing in all creation is hidden from God. Everything is naked and exposed before his eyes, and he is the one to whom we are accountable." Hebrews 4:13

Jumping for Joy

"Jesus Christ is the same yesterday and today and forever." Hebrews 13:8

"For his anger is but for a moment, and his favor is for a lifetime. Weeping may tarry for the night, but joy comes with the morning." Psalm 30:5

"So also you have sorrow now, but I will see you again, and your hearts will rejoice, and no one will take your joy from you." John 16:22

Take a Risk

"But the Helper, the Holy Spirit, whom the Father will send in my name, he will teach you all things and bring to your remembrance all that I have said to you." John 14:26

"Peace I leave with you; my peace I give to you. Not as the world gives do I give to you. Let not your hearts be troubled, neither let them be afraid."

John 14:27

.."for God gave us a spirit not of fear but of power and love and self-control." 2 Timothy 1:7

Freedom

"Then he said to Thomas, "Put your finger here; see my hands. Reach   out your hand and put it into my side. Stop doubting and believe." John 20:27

"But he was pierced for our transgressions, he was crushed for our iniquities; the punishment that brought us peace was on him, and by his wounds we are healed." Isaiah 53:5

"And I am sure of this, that he who began a good work in you will bring it to completion at the day of Jesus Christ." Philippians 1:6

Daughter

"When you pass through the waters, I will be with you; and when you pass through the rivers, they will not sweep over you. When you walk through the fire, you will not be burned; the flames will not set you ablaze." Isaiah 43:2

"See what great love the Father has lavished on us, that we should be called children of God! And that is what we are!" 1 John 3:1

"She is clothed with strength and dignity, and she laughs without fear of the future." Proverbs 31:25

Connect with Us:

Our time has come to an end, but you are never alone. We want to say connected to you through our Beautifully Designed community! This online community is made up of more than 20,000 women from all walks of life and backgrounds who come together regularly to pray, study the Scriptures, and give one another hope as each discovers their true identity in Christ. For direction on how to join our community and learn more about Ashley's first book (Beautifully Designed), visit www.beautifullydesigned.com.

If you would like to connect to Ashley and the Beautifully Designed ministry team, you may do so at www.beautifullydesigned.com/contact. We love hearing how God is transforming lives through this ministry!

About the Author:

Ashley Shepherd is a wife, mother, entrepreneur, public speaker, published author, and minister to women. The daughter of a preacher, she was born and raised in East Tennessee, where she lives today with husband, Ryan, and their two boys. In the fall of 2015, Ashley launched an online Bible study that quickly grew to more than 9,000 women in the first month. Today, the Beautifully Designed community reaches over 20,000 women across the world through Bible studies, the Beautifully Designed podcast, and community projects. Whether you plan a women's conference or gather a small group, Ashley loves to speak to groups of all sizes and ages. Her communication style is marked by a down-to-earth tone and relatable transparency as she presents a message of hope for women in every season of life. If you would like to bring her to your community, we invite you to, www.beautifullydesigned.com/speaking. No event is too large or too small.

Made in the USA
Columbia, SC
06 April 2019